SECRETS OF MY SOUL

By

D. M. Larson

Contact doug@freedrama.net for
performance permission or
questions about the scripts.

SECRETS OF MY SOUL BY D. M. LARSON

Dedicated to my wife, my best friend and my muse, Shiela Larson.  Thank you for your love and inspiration.

\* \* \* \* \* \* \* \* \* \*

"We laugh our smiles and weep our tears, even argue, fight and share our fears. You know the secrets of my soul, you fill its emptiness, you make me whole...." - anonymous

\* \* \* \* \* \* \* \* \* \*

INTRODUCTION

This script is a series of short plays and monologues.  The producer of the play may select some or all of the scripts for the performance.  As a way to tie the scripts together, all actors from the production can appear in the scene "The Fire" to start the play to set the stage for the upcoming scenes.

PART 1


"THE FIRE"

(Lights in this play are dim to show darkness. A blue tint to the lights might add to the effect. On stage are several cots with people sleeping on them. TANDE enters cautiously among the sleeping people. He reaches about center and is distracted by a sudden loud snore behind him. This causes him to run into a cot, C)

          SLEEPER
Who's that?  What's with knockin' my bed?

          SHOUTER
Quiet!

          SLEEPER
Quiet yourself.

          TANDE
I'm sorry. Please go back to sleep.

          SLEEPER
Don't you start tellin' me what to do. You done plenty already.

(CONTINUED)

                    TANDE
It was an accident.

                    SHOUTER
Will you shut up?!

                    WHINER
Hey, man. Go to sleep. There's
other people around here ya' know.

                    SLEEPER
Shut your trap.

                    TANDE
Please, all of you, go back to
sleep.

                    SWEET
Who's the fancy talker?

                    SLEEPER
They ain't nobody.  Anybody come
here is nobody now.

                    TANDE
I'm sorry. I just need a place to
sleep.

                    SLEEPER
There ain't a place for you here.

                    SWEET
You got two cots. Why don't you
give him one?

                    SLEEPER
What with you? You take a likin' to
him?

                    SWEET
He seems nice.  I'd like him to
stay.

                    SLEEPER
I ain't got no cot.

                    TANDE
I'll go. It's okay.

                    SWEET
You can always sleep with me,
honey, I got lots of room.

> SHOUTER
> What're you talkin' about? You're
> the one who needs two cots for that
> big backside of yours.

> SWEET
> Careful what you say, I might cry.

> WHINER
> Oh, man. Last time she cry, she
> wouldn't shut up all night.

> TANDE
> Everyone, please. I didn't mean to
> cause so much trouble.

> SLEEPER
> You too late. You already did. Now,
> you have to pay.

> SWEET
> (Almost a whisper)
> Be gentle with him.

> SLEEPER
> Shut up, woman!

> SHOUTER
> Why don't you?! I'm tryin' to sleep
> here.

(Silence. SLEEPER crosses to SHOUTER's bed. He stands over
him a moment)

> SHOUTER (CONT.)
> What do you want?!

> SLEEPER
> No one mouths off at me.

> SHOUTER
> Too late, I already did.

(In a quick motion, SLEEPER tips the cot, kicks SHOUTER, and
pins him to the floor with his foot. TANDE tries to escape L
during this but is caught by WHINER. WHINER pushes TANDE
roughly into a sitting position on a cot. Once again
everything is still again)

> SLEEPER
> What you say to me, boy?

                    SHOUTER
Nothin', nothin' at all.

                    SLEEPER
And what you say to me later?

                    SHOUTER
Nothin'.

                    WHINER
           (Holding TANDE)
I got this one.

                    WHINER
What you gonna do with him?

(SLEEPER Crosses to TANDE, grabs his face roughly and makes
TANDE look up at him)

                    SLEEPER
Does I scare you?

                    TANDE
           (Softly)
Yes.

(SLEEPER smiles, still holding TANDE, looking into his
eyes.  TANDE is terrified, certain he is about to die)

                    SLEEPER
It's that look I love. I loves it
more than women. And you's got it.

(SLEEPER roughly releases TANDE. Others leave him alone and
go to the corners to converse. SLEEPER sits on his cot.
SWEET goes to TANDE)

                    SWEET
Hi, there.

                    TANDE
Hi.

                    SWEET
My name's Sweet.

(Holds out hand. They shake)

                    TANDE
Tande.

                                    (CONTINUED)

                         SWEET
          I think Sleeper likes you.

                         TANDE
          I think you're wrong.

                         SWEET
          He's not as bad as he looks. He's
          really a pussy cat deep down.

                         TANDE
          Yeah, with long claws, long teeth,
          and rabies.

                         SWEET
          Oh, you're funny. I like you.

(SLEEPER moves in closer and TANDE brushes off the unwanted
intimacy)

                         TANDE
          Where am I?

(SHOUTER joins them)

                         WHINER
          You're down, man. You're at the end
          of existence.

                         SWEET
          He exaggerates.

                         WHINER
          You eg-za-der-dates if you's sayin'
          otherwise.

                         TANDE
          I was told to come here. At least,
          I think this is the place.
               ((Takes out paper))
          Here's the address.

(SWEET is silent when he sees paper)

                         WHINER
          That's bad man. Real bad.

                         TANDE
          What is?

                         WHINER
          That place.

                                                   (CONTINUED)

                    TANDE
          Then this isn't it?


                    WHINER
          This place is far from it, man.
          This is Disneyland to that.


                    TANDE
          Maybe I shouldn't go.


                    SWEET
          You have to.


                    TANDE
          How do I get there?


                    WHINER
          Sleeper can take you.


                    TANDE
          Sleeper? Why him?


                    WHINER
          That's a bad place. Only Sleeper
          goes there. They say he's from that
          neighborhood.


                    SWEET
          If that's possible.  How can anyone
          be from that place?


                    TANDE
          Can it be that bad?


                    WHINER
          Where you comin' from, man? Don't
          you know nothin' about this
          neighborhood?


                    TANDE
          This is all new to me.


                    WHINER
          It better be unnew and fast or
          you's gonna lose yourself here.


                    SWEET
          That place where you're going...


                    TANDE
          Yeah?

                    SWEET
It's dangerous... cops don't even
go there.

                    WHINER
And when Sleeper goes, he don't
bring no one back.

                    SWEET
You didn't have to tell him that.

                    WHINER
It's the truth, ain't it?

                    TANDE
I just won't go then. I'll stay
here. That's easy enough.

                    WHINER
You forget. Sleeper won't let you.

                    TANDE
Damned if I do, damned if I don't.

                    WHINER
Hey, he catches on quick.

                    SWEET
Not quick enough I'm afraid.

                    TANDE
Won't Sleeper help me through?

                    WHINER
Sleeper? Help? Those words don't go
together, man. Sleeper would sooner
see you hurt than helped. That's
his way.

                    TANDE
I may as well go alone then.

                    SWEET
Sleeper would go anyway. It's his
job. You may as well go with him.

                    WHINER
It'll be quicker... if that
matters.

                    TANDE
I don't understand any of this.
What is this stupid address?  Why
                    (MORE)

                    TANDE (cont'd)
          can't I remember how I go it?  I
          don't want to go, but what else can
          I do? There's nothing behind me.
          There's nothing here. The only
          thing I have is this address.

                    WHINER
          It could be worse...

                    SLEEPER
          Could it?

(Moment of silence. SLEEPER gets up and puts on a jacket.
SLEEPER crosses over to them. WHINER seeshim and crosses
away. TANDE and SWEET notice SLEEPER when WHINER leaves)

                    SLEEPER
                ((To TANDE))
          You comin'?

(TANDE looks to SWEET pleadingly)

                    SWEET
          You'd better go.

(SWEET gets up and crosses away)

                    SLEEPER
          Show me your paper.

                    TANDE
          Paper?

                    SLEEPER
                ((Louder and sharper))
          The address!

(TANDE quickly gives it to him)

                    SLEEPER
                ((Laughs darkly))
          Bad place. What's a fancy talkin'
          little wuss like you doin' in a
          neighborhood like this?

                    TANDE
          I wish I could remember... I think
          someone gave me the address. I
          don't remember them saying anything
          else.

                         SLEEPER
          Probably better that way.

                         TANDE
          What is this place anyway?

                         SLEEPER
          That depends on you.

                         TANDE
          What is that supposed to mean?

                         SLEEPER
               ((Laughs))
          You see soon 'nough. What that they
          say. "Patience is a..." What's that
          word?

                         TANDE
          "Virtue."

                         SLEEPER
          Yeah. You got to get yourself some
          of that.

                         TANDE
          I thought I had plenty before this.

                         SLEEPER
          You find you got a lot less after.

(Starts to exit)

                         SLEEPER (CONT.)
          It's time.

(SWEET goes up to TANDE)

                         SWEET
          Keep safe.

                         SLEEPER
          I ain't got the time!

                         SWEET
          You'd better go.

                         TANDE
          Good-bye. Perhaps I'll be back this
          way again.

(SWEET smiles sadly and turns and cries.  WHINER rolls his
eyes)

(CONTINUED)

                    SLEEPER
          You comin'?

(TANDE follows SLEEPER off R. SWEET watches sadly. WHINER
glances reluctantly, but turns away. Lights fade to black)

END OF SCENE

* * * * * * * * * * * *

PART 2


"THE NOT SO PERFECT CHILD" - MONOLOGUE- FEMALE

                    MOIRA

(Quiet anger)
          You hate me don't you? I am never
          good enough for you.

(Anger builds)
          No matter what I do it's not as
          good as my sister.  I always have
          to hear how she would have done it
          better.  Or how she already did it
          better.

(Hurt)
          Why does she want to ruin my
          life?  She just wants to blot me
          out like I was some sort of
          mistake... I'm just a copy... A
          copy of a copy... Not as good as
          the original... Not as good as you.

(Sarcastic and bitter)
          You are so perfect... Everyone
          around me is so perfect... And
          there was nothing left over for
          me... I am the leftover failures...
          I am the fatty waste you toss to
          the dogs.

(Fury)
          Everyone hates me!  Why does
          everyone think I am so horrible...
          (Shakes and tries to hold back the
          fury) Probably because I am.  A
          horrible creature doomed to walk
          this earth and suffer... For you.

(Cries uncontrollably... Struggles to speak)


                                              (CONTINUED)

I'm hurting... Hurting so bad
inside.  Cut off from everyone ...
Punished for some past life
wrongs... What did I do in a past
life to deserve this... Or am I
paying for the sins of my father...
And mother... Am I your sin?  Or do
I remind you of some sin you want
to forget?

(Anger builds)
Or I am a disappointment that keeps
disappointing.  I even disappoint
myself.

(Furious)
I will never be my sister.  I don't
to be her.  I hate everything about
her!

(Cries... Sadness)
But I don't want to be me
either.  Sometimes I want to fade
away... Become a shadow... Fading
away... Forgotten... Maybe if you
forget about me I won't make you so
sad anymore.

(She hears a knock at her door.  She tries to fix her up ...
Wipes away the tears)
What's that mom ?  I was just
watching a video... Was it too
loud?  I'm sorry.... I'm really
sorry.

END OF SCENE

* * * * * * * * * * *

PART 3


"CONFESSION"

Lights are dim and focus on a corner of the church which the
confessional.  We see Jude and Delia but they are divided by
a partition.

                    DELIA
          I'm scared, Father.


                                               (CONTINUED)

                         JUDE
Scared?  Of what?

                         DELIA
Everything.

                         JUDE
God will protect you.

                         DELIA
I wish I could believe that.

                         JUDE
You can trust God.

                         DELIA
I fear God. I don't trust him.  I
am afraid what he is going to
do.  I am afraid of what will
happen every day... If I go
outside, what will be waiting for
me?  There's something wrong out
there.  Something's not right.

                         JUDE
Things are changing.  I have sensed
it too.

                         DELIA
What do we do?

                         JUDE
Trust in God.

                         DELIA
Back to that again... How can I
trust him?  How can I trust the
one who took my father away? How
can I trust the one who turned my
mother into a drunk? How I trust
the one who put me in the house of
someone who abused me?  Every day I
lived in fear.  What would happen
if I stepped outside my room?  I
didn't know what was waiting for
me.  I never knew what would wake
up that day.  The creep, the angry
one, the monster... I didn't even
want to get out of bed anymore.  It
got too hard.  I was too scared.  I
would hide and pray to God to help
me.  But God never did.  My
childhood gone and my only escape
was adulthood.

                                        (CONTINUED)

JUDE
You blamed God for all that?

DELIA
Even if God didn't do it why did he
let it happen?

JUDE
He will never give you more than
you can handle.

DELIA
I can't handle it though... I'm
going crazy.. The fear is crippling
me... I have to drag myself out of
bed and force myself to live each
day... Sure, I put on this happy
face... People think I am pretty
cheerful... No one cares to see the
pain under my skin... The pain
that's ripping at my soul.

JUDE
God sees.

DELIA
I know.

JUDE
Have you sinned?

DELIA
What?

JUDE
Are you a sinner?

DELIA
I don't know...

JUDE
Do you think about sinning?

DELIA
All the time.

JUDE
What stops you?

DELIA
Fear... Fear of what might happen
to me... See, I'm afraid of
everything.

                    JUDE
Your fear could be a blessing.

                    DELIA
What?

                    JUDE
It keeps you from doing wrong... It
keep you from doing anything evil.

                    DELIA
I hope so.

                    JUDE
Do you feel tempted?

                    DELIA
All the time.

                    JUDE
What tempts you?

                    DELIA
I'm tempted to give up... It's too
hard to keep living.

                    JUDE
Perhaps you need something to live
for.

                    DELIA
I do.

                    JUDE
We will ask God to give you
something to live for... We are all
born with a purpose.

                    DELIA
I just want to know what it is.

END OF SCENE

* * * * * * * * * * *

PART 4

"DEAR GOD"

(BILLY is an adult who exhibits child-like behavior. He gathers a notepad and goes to get a pencil and sharpens it with a small hand sharpener)

                    BILLY
          A pencil has to be just right.
          Never too sharp, never too dull. If
          it's too sharp it might poke me and
          I'll get lead poisoning and die! I
          saw a show about that once. People
          dying of lead... oh, yes and going
          nuts. I seem to remember Van Gogh
          got so much lead poisoning he cut
          off his ear! Ouch! That's like out
          of Shakespeare... friends, Romans,
          countrymen! Lend me your ears! Ha!

(Checking the pencil. Pokes him)
          Ouch! Too sharp...

(Tosses the pencil. Starts on another)
          Now let's try to be a bit dull...
          dullness has it's merits. You can't
          get hurt. People don't expect as
          much from you. You do the job, but
          never for too long.

(Checks pencil. Smiles)
          Dull it is.

(Sits with pad and paper)
          Now, we're ready.

(Pauses as if listening to someone)
          I know, I know... I will address it
          to Mr. God. You've nagged me a
          million times about this. I know!
          Just, just give me time okay. This
          is an important letter so I don't
          want to rush it, okay.

(Starts to write)
          Dear God, I seem to have found
          something that is yours. A few
          nights ago, I was in bed, sleeping
          I think, and then she was there.
          She was at my bedside, all white
          and glowing, rocking in my
          grannie's old chair. I couldn't
          really look at her though. She was
                    (MORE)

                              BILLY (cont'd)
              all bright like the sun, giving me
              those spots on my eyes, those ones
              you have to blink away until their
              gone. I must say I was a bit scared
              and threw the covers over my head.
              When I looked again, she was still
              there! I couldn't believe it. I
              said, "You're hurting my eyes."
              Kind of a silly thing to say. Why
              didn't I say, "Are you a ghost?" or
              something a bit smarter? She said
              she was sorry and vanished. I was
              worried I'd licked a few too many
              pencils and was going to cut off my
              ear, but then I heard her voice.
              She told me how she had fallen and
              couldn't get back home. Her wings
              were broken and she couldn't fly.
              "Are you an angel?" I asked her.
              She said she was. I told her she
              could stay. See, I don't have many
              people here, just Mom. I thought
              she could hang out with me. She
              said yes, but now Mom wants her to
              go away. She said it's not good for
              me to be talking to her. I thought
              mom liked angels but I guess not.
              Anyway... can you send a car around
              or a winged chariot or something to
              pick her up? She wants to come home
              now. Sincerely, Billy Graham.

(Giggles)
              I wonder if God will know which
              Billy Graham is writing him? I bet
              it will get his attention, that's
              for sure.

(Looks at letter)
              Now how do I send this? Does God
              have a P.O. box? Is it like Santa
              Clause... you know, Santa, North
              Pole... God, Heaven...

(Listens to voice)
              What? Burn the letter? Why? Will
              that work? If you say so.

(Goes to a cabinet)
              Mom hides the matches from me.
              They're over here.

(Pulls out box of matches)

            I think there's a reason she does.

(Gets out an ashtray)
            I got this from Motel 6. Nice huh?
            I collect these things. Every time
            Grampa used to take me somewhere,
            I'd get one. No, they're free. They
            have all kinds of free stuff in
            motel rooms: pens, notepads, and
            towels. Grampa liked it all. He
            said he always wanted to get his
            money's worth.

END OF SCENE

* * * * * * * * * * *

PART 5


"DEATH TAKES THE TRAIN"

A train car is empty.  Groups of people shuffle in and
settle in to seats to the right.  People are talking about
their trips and their destinations and how tired or hungry
they are.  Then after a pause, the Grim Reaper walks on to
the train and sits alone at the left side of the train car.

                    MEL
            Is that who I think it is?

                    MITCH
            I think so.

                    MEL
            What's he doing on this train?

                    TINA
            How do you know it's a he?

                    MEL
            Death is always a guy.

                    TINA
            Always?

                    MEL
            I think so.

                    TINA
            But he's wearing a dress.

                    MITCH
          Or is more of a moo-moo.

                    MEL
          Robe... it's a robe.  Guys can wear
          robes.

                    TINA
          After a shower.

                    MITCH
          Or if they are some kind of judge.

                    TINA
          Death is a like a judge.

                    MEL
          True... I see what you mean.

                    TINA
          A justice of the peace?

                    MITCH
          A justice of rest in peace.

                    TINA
          Nice one.

                    MITCH
          Thanks.

                    TINA
          You're welcome.

                    MITCH
          So what's he doing here?

                    TINA
          He's got a client I guess.

                    MEL
          One of us?

                    TINA
          No, he's probably on his way
          somewhere.

                    MITCH
          Why is death taking the train?

                    MEL
          His winged horse o' death didn't
          have the guts to go there... get
                    (MORE)

                    MEL (cont'd)
it... because it's a skeleton
horse... no guts...

                    TINA
Please don't explain the
joke.  It's not funny if you have
to explain it.

                    MEL
Geez... I'll just let Mitch make
all the jokes then.

                    TINA
Thank you.

                    MITCH
You're welcome.

                    TINA
Death taking the train doesn't make
any sense.  Doesn't that take too
long?  Wouldn't death be in more of
a hurry?

                    MITCH
Maybe not... modern medicine is
keeping people alive longer.  Maybe
he's not in a hurry anymore.

                    MEL
Maybe he's on a tight budget like
the rest of us.  The bad economy is
even affecting life and death.

                    TINA
I like Mitch's theory better.

                    MEL
Of course you do.

                    TINA
Mitch has a point.  People aren't
dying as quick as they used to or
as often.  Modern medicine can keep
people alive for years beyond what
normally would kill them.

                    MEL
So Death saves money and takes the
train.

                    MITCH
And he's being very environmentally
aware too.  Trains burn much less
energy than planes and cars.  Death
is doing his part to help the
Earth.

                    MEL
Wouldn't Death like pollution?

                    TINA
Not necessarily.  Maybe he likes
the natural order of things.  Maybe
he's doing what he can to help
restore the balance that people
offset through technological
advancements.

                    MITCH
Well said.

                    TINA
Thank you.

                    MITCH
I wonder where Death takes people?

                    MEL
To the H-E-double hockey sticks
place down below.

                    TINA
What if they're good?

                    MEL
Heaven.

                    MITCH
Wouldn't that be an angel then?

                    TINA
We're all assuming there is a
heaven...

                    MITCH
I'd like to think there is.

                    MEL
It's nicer that way... thinking
there is someplace good we go if we
lived a good life.  And that bad
people are punished for being bad.

(CONTINUED)

                         TINA
          But who decides what is good and
          what is bad?

                         MEL
          God.

                         TINA
          What if you don't believe in God?

                         MEL
          That's okay.  God still believes in
          you.

                         TINA
          I'd feel a whole lot better facing
          death if I knew for sure.

                         MITCH
          Just the fact that we see Death
          sitting over there gives me hope
          that there is something more beyond
          life.

                         TINA
          Wow, who would have thought seeing
          Death would make you feel
          hopeful?  That's some serious
          optimism you got there, Mitch.

                         MITCH
          I wonder if he would talk to
          us.  I'd love to ask him about all
          this.  Life after death... good vs.
          evil...

                         MEL
          He doesn't look like much of a
          talker.   And what if he speaks
          Latin or Ewok or something like
          that?

                         TINA
          Ewok?

                         MEL
          I'm just making a point that he
          might be from somewhere else.

                         TINA
          I'd go with Latin over Ewok.

                    MITCH
          Or maybe he has a universal
          translator that helps him
          understand all languages.

                    TINA
          That would make sense.

                    MEL
          No it doesn't... none of this
          does.  Doesn't it strike you as
          weird that we've never seen death
          before?

                    TINA
          True.  I've never seen him before.

                    MITCH
          You don't think that means...

                    MEL
          What happened to Mr. Optimism?

                    MITCH
          He jumped the train.

                    TINA
          Do you think he could be here for
          us?

                    MITCH
          All of us?

They pause.  They look at Death and then each other
nervously.  They're all quiet a moment thinking.  Tina chews
some gum... blows a bubble and the other three jump when it
pops.

                    MEL
          Do you think the train could be
          crashing or something?

                    MITCH
          That's the only way I can see all
          of us dying.

                    TINA
          Should we warn the conductor?

                    MEL
          We could get off at the next
          station.

> MITCH
> Or maybe we should face Death head
> on without fear.

Mitch stands and the others huddle in fear.  Mitch takes a
few steps toward Death but then slows as he gets closer.  He
starts to choke and stumble.  The others rush to him and
help him back to their side of the car.

> MEL
> What happened?

> TINA
> It's like he couldn't breathe.

Mitch nods.

> TINA (CONT.)
> Like the air around him is deadly.

> MEL
> So much for talking to Death.

> TINA
> Are you okay Mitch?

Mitch nods again.

> MEL
> What's the matter?  Did he talk you
> to death?  Death got your tongue?

> TINA
> Not funny, Mel.

> MEL
> Come on... my jokes that bad?

> TINA
> Let's just say they bore me to
> death.

> MEL
> (Sarcastic)
> Funny.

> TINA
> Jealous?

> MEL
> No.

                    MITCH
          Remind me not to do that again.

                    TINA
          What did he do you?

                    MITCH
          Nothing directly I don't
          think.  It's like the air around
          him is deadly.

                    MEL
          Maybe Death farted or something.

                    TINA
          Care to go see?

                    MEL
          No, that's okay... so what are we
          going to do?

                    TINA
          How far is the next station?  We
          could get off.

                    MEL
          Wait... what if we're already dead
          and Death is the conductor?

                    TINA
          We could test that theory at the
          next station.  Let's get ready to
          get off.

                    MITCH
          You all can get off... I'm
          staying.  I have somewhere to be
          and I can't be late.

                    TINA
          What if Death is here for you
          though?  Then you won't make it
          anyway.

                    MITCH
          If he's not here for us then we
          waste a lot of time by getting
          off.

                    TINA
          I think I'd rather gamble with
          being late than dead.

> MEL
> Here's the next station... I'm
> going.

Mel gets up and the train stops so he stumbles to the
ground.

> TINA
> Wait until the train stops, idiot.

> MEL
> I'm not dead am I?

> TINA
> Afraid not.

TINA helps Mel up and Mel heads off the train.

> TINA (CONT.)
> Come on, Mitch.  Please.

> MITCH
> I can't miss my kid's birthday.  I
> promised her.  She's counting on
> me.

> TINA
> Okay, Mitch.  Take care of
> yourself.

> MITCH
> I will.

Tina exits and then it is only Mitch and Death.

> MITCH (CONT.)
> So Death... what's it going to be?

After a pause, Death gets up and follows the others.  Mitch
stands and is scared.  He rushes to the window and faces the
audience and looks out in fear for his friends.

END OF SCENE

* * * * * * * * * * *

PART 6

"GHOSTS I'VE KNOWN"

                    EMILY
Ghosts have always been with
me.  Not by choice.  At least not
on my part.  It just happens.  I
don't want to believe... but
they've forced themselves on me.
(Thoughtful)
Perhaps the old Indian woman did it
to me.  I lived in her house too
long as a child.
(Looks at ceiling)
At night, footsteps paced the
ceiling.  Over and over, an
impatient march, forever in step to
the silent drum.  If only this had
been my only encounter, I could
dismiss it.  "The house is
settling," my mother said... but
this wasn't all the house did.
(Lights slightly flicker)
Lights dimmed and glowed.  Her
ghostly will stronger than the new
world magic conjured by
GE.  Sometimes she preferred a
blackout.  She didn't care for my
brother's taste in
music.  Blackout!
(Blackout)
My brother was scared turdless.
(Lights come up dimly again.  She
smiles at the memory of her
brother.  She is thoughtful a
moment and her expression darkens)
These spirits are on me like dogs
on turds.  Always sniffing
around.  Marking me.
(Goes to sofa.  Sits and slowly
makes her way under the quilt and
lays her head sleepily against the
back of the sofa during the
following)
I slept in my room.  Well, not
really slept.  Sleep was never
something I did much of, especially
early on.  My worries at seven far
outweighed my need for
sleep.  Awake.  Forever
awake.  My father had left
me.  My mother...
(Sits up.  Then gets up and crosses
to coffin)
                    (MORE)

(CONTINUED)

                              EMILY (cont'd)
I was always worried mother would
leave me too.
(She touches the coffin
lovingly.  Then stops looking very
tired)
I wish the ghosts would go.  But
they linger.  Always
lingering.  Never really gone.
(She goes to rocking chair and
pushes it with her hand so it
rocks.  She crosses to sofa and
sits staring at the rocking chair)
The old Indian woman was my
first.  She rocked at my beside,
all in white.  My eyes met
hers.  Her eyes giving me a worried
look as if I were the one who had
expired.
(Slowly slips quilt over
herself.  Holds it up so she can't
see rocker, but audience can still
see her)
Fear making my head sink deeply
into covers.  My eyes entombed by
my lids.  How long she waited, I'll
never know.  By dawn I ventured a
look.  She was gone... or perhaps
she was never there.
(Lowers covers)
Thinking the apparition a dream, I
told my family and their eyes
betrayed them.  Others had known
her too.
(Rises from bed)
Mother had a vision.  She did not
go questing for it though.  The
old Indian, young to most who saw
her, once lived on this land.  A
servant.  A girl died here, she at
her side...  at her side rocking...
and the girl died.
(Stoking coffin)
And then I died too...
(Waits for reaction, then smiles)
Not really... I just wanted to see
your reaction... but it certainly
would have made for a dramatic
twist in my tale.  A Poeish twist
for you to savor.  But I lived on.
(Looking at coffin)
I wish I could say the same for
you...
                    (MORE)

>                    EMILY (cont'd)
> (Growing worried)
> Spirits dog me.  Just when I no
> longer believe, they
> appear.  Flashing white lights.   A
> cold touch.   They return.
> (Shivers)
> Even now.
> (Smiles)
> The haunted RV.   Sounds like a bad
> horror paperback for kids.   Wish
> it had been.   RV's are spirit
> magnets, you know, easier to tackle
> than a home.   Perhaps I would
> choose an RV too.   An eternity on
> the road rather than an eternity at
> home.   A RV ghost would never be a
> homebody.
> (Thoughtful)
> Actually they can't be a
> homebody... no body.
> (Looks for reaction.  Sighs)
> Ouch.  Sorry.  Bad joke.
> (Back to story)
> Strange things happen to me in
> RVs.   The first time was in
> battle.   A battle between
> brothers.   A bloody battle of
> battered bodies, literally torn
> limb from limb... or so I read in
> the visitor's center orientation
> pamphlets.
> (Scans the room with an imaginary
> digital camera)
> I scanned the graveyard with my
> digital eye, scanning the graves
> until I spotted one.   A misty form
> hovering over a tombstone, my
> unaided eyes not seeing, the
> digital Cyclops screaming in
> revelation... then
> blackout.  Power gone,
> interrupted.   I switched in on
> again and took a picture, capturing
> whatever it was.   Capturing more
> than I knew.
> (Looks around)
> After that, so many strange things
> happened in the RV, mostly the
> fan.   The fan kept turning on by
> itself.   Spinning and
> spinning.   Where it stops
> nobody... or spirit...
>                    (MORE)

                              EMILY (cont'd)
knows.    Finally, I asked it to
stop and it did.    This is when the
real fear set in.
(Thoughtful)
Fear?  No, not fear.   So often had
I encountered these things that I
didn't have that "run away and
scream" fear.   It was casual
curiosity, bordering on fascination
fear.  I could never flee from
learning.
(Expression grows dark)
But this time it was too
much.   Another RV.   Another
place.   Another spirit.   This
time it was someone I knew.
(Sadness as she returns to
coffin.  Slowly turns to panic
during following)
It started with the call.  The news
that she had gone away.  Finding
myself in tears.  Tears sapping me
dry.  Would the tears ever
stop?  Pain like a thick metal pole
shoved up your ass.  But the ass
wouldn't like it.   Braying and
wounded, unable to pack the
burden.  It's long ears drooping,
it's tail missing.   Call
Christopher Robin.   We need help!
(Tries to calm herself)
I had lost so much.   An emptiness
replaces love, anxious to find,
nothing there... no body anyway,
but something.   Something that
opens doors, something leaving
tissue by the bed.   The dog
barking at nothing... but
something.   Finding things in new
places, things missing.   The
locked door... open.
(Tries to calm herself)
Explanations fly.   Knowledge our
protection.   Education like a
condom for the unknown.
(Grins)
Pardon my similes.  Sometimes I
amuse myself.
(Thinks a moment.  Frowns and
shivers)
It began with the cold.   Spots of
cold.  A moment of normal then
                    (MORE)

                    EMILY (cont'd)
cold, as if the heat were sucked
into another dimension.  These
don't bother me as much as the
touch.   A handless touch of
nothing.  Something grabbed by arm
but no one was there.
(Pulls back in fear and runs for
sofa)
To Hades with explorations,
knowledge or condoms... I ran for
bed, buried myself in covers and
waited for dawn.
(Throws covers overhead.  Pause)
You're never too old to hide under
the covers.  Wrapping yourself up
into a cocoon.  Hoping that when
you emerge life will be butterflies
again.
(She sighs and sits up)
But only children believe in
butterflies.
(She rises again)
Adults know... or learn... that
life is full of moths,
caterpillars, and worms.
(Sings softly)
"The worms crawl in, the worms
crawl out, the worms play pinochle
in your snout."
(A loud thump off stage makes her
stop.  She is frozen a moment then
continues)
Like Ebenezer, I wish these spooks
would leave me.
(Pause)
But when I'm alone... fear sets
in.   I wonder... do I really want
to be alone?  Maybe their visits
comfort me.
(Goes to coffin)
Was it you that touched me that
day?
(Sadly)
And if you are still here, why do I
feel so alone?
(Lights fade to black.  The rocker
is heard again creaking as it
rocks)


END OF SCENE

* * * * * * * * * * *

PART 7


"SIRENS AT SEA"

Odysseus stands on the deck of a ship near the main mast
with heavy rope.  One of his soldiers runs up to him.

                    SOLDIER
          What are you doing, Odysseus?

                    ODYSSEUS
          Get all the men below.

                    SOLDIER
          You can't stay up here.

                    ODYSSEUS
          Someone must.

                    SOLDIER
          You can't do this.  No one
          survives.  Come below.

                    ODYSSEUS
          No.  This is something I need to
          do.

                    SOLDIER
          I'll stay with you then.  We'll
          face them together.

                    ODYSSEUS
          Get below!  That's an order.

                    SOLDIER
          You're mad.

                    ODYSSEUS
          I have to do this.  We'll never
          escape if I don't.

                    SOLDIER
          What are you talking about?

                    ODYSSEUS
          He'll never release us unless I
          face them.  We'll never escape this
          storm until I do.  Tie me to the
          mast.

                                        (CONTINUED)

                         SOLDIER
               Tie you?

                         ODYSSEUS
               They say the Sirens' song drive men
               to madness and they cast themselves
               in the sea.  If I'm bound, I won't
               be able to flee.

                         SOLDIER
               But the madness...

                         ODYSSEUS
               He drove me to madness long ago.

                         SOLDIER
               He?

                         ODYSSEUS
               I can't say his name.

                         SOLDIER
               Damn the gods.

                         ODYSSEUS
               Hurry and bind me and get
               below.  Lock yourselves in and
               don't come out until the storm
               ends.

          Soldier ties up Odysseus.

                         SOLDIER
               May we see each other again soon.

                         ODYSSEUS
               May you live to tell the tale.

          Soldier runs below.  Odysseus closes his eyes.

                         ODYSSEUS (CONT.)
               I face this test like all
               others.  I resist as I always
               resist.  Though you drive me to
               madness, I survive.  You hear
               me?!  I survive!  (a long silence)
               ...but what is survival without
               reward... what is survival with
               emptiness... I could have kept to
               the safety of the shore, the
               security of my home... but there
               was so much emptiness... and I
               never found the reward despite all
                         (MORE)

                              ODYSSEUS (CONT.) (cont'd)
              my labors... I slowly felt myself
              slipping away... but the sea... the
              sea and the battles that awaited
              me... will they destroy me?  Was I
              not prepared for what I would
              face?  Did I wait too long to take
              up my sword?  Am I too weak
              now?  Did I let my best years fade
              from me while keeping house?  I
              love my children but did I fade as
              they grew?  Did I trade ambition
              for children's games?  Am I now
              lost because I wasn't strong enough
              to be anything but a nurse
              maid?  Where am I?  Where have I
              gone?  I'm lost at sea and lost
              inside myself?  Give me
              direction!  Give me an answer!  I
              need something!  Anything!  Why
              have you cast me out again?!  Am I
              lost in my madness for all
              eternity?!

The sounds of the storm fade and are replaced by a haunting
sound of singing.  Two women's voices are heard.  SARA and
RACHEL are two women that are bird-like in appearance,
cloaked and hooded in feathers.  One is dark (SARA) and the
other is light (RACHEL).

                    SARA
              You sail the sea for thousand days,
              you sail the sea for a thousand
              more, lost forever and without
              love, you miss the embrace of
              eternal night.

                    RACHEL
              But you search no more, your answer
              has come... Come with me and be
              reborn, come with me and never
              mourn.  I will heal the heart
              that's torn.

Each time the other is speaking one pulls at the ropes that
bind him to the mast.  The storm gets calmer and calmer.

                    SARA
              The journey's end is close to you,
              no more weary days to view, you
              can't hold on to life no more, you
              will serve the night once more.

                         RACHEL
          Come to me and feel the light, the
          lightness of my appetite, I crave
          for you and will crave me, I will
          cloud your worries and dull the
          pains, the pains which stab your
          heart and slowly destroy your life.


                         SARA
          Life has ended and gives you no
          hope, so follow me in to the night.


                         RACHEL
          I bring you light that blinds the
          sorrow which fills your heart.

They pull the ropes from him and he falls to their feet.

                         ODYSSEUS
          Who are you?  You both know
          me.  Who are my tormentors?

There is a sudden darkness.  Sara stands over him and Rachel
is gone.  Sara has dropped her feather robe and now looks
like a queen and has placed a crown on her head.  Odysseus
looks up shocked.

                         ODYSSEUS (CONT.)
          Penelope?

                         SARA/PENELOPE
          Do you come here to serve me? Or
          beg forgiveness?

                         ODYSSEUS
          Is it really you, my wife?  My
          Penelope?

                         SARA/PENELOPE
          Do you believe what you see?

                         ODYSSEUS
          It's been so long... my eyes are
          tired.

                         SARA/PENELOPE
          And I grow tired of you.

                         ODYSSEUS
          I'm sorry, Penelope.  I don't see
          what I did.

> SARA/PENELOPE
> Then what's the point of talking.

> ODYSSEUS
> Why are you so angry?

> SARA/PENELOPE
> I grow tired of you playing warrior
> and your travels.  I want you
> close, to fulfill your role as my
> husband and rule with me.

> ODYSSEUS
> I grew restless.  Do you wish for
> me to keep planning feasts and
> raising children when I am needed
> elsewhere?

> SARA/PENELOPE
> You are needed here.  Don't you
> wish to serve your home?

> ODYSSEUS
> I wish to be useful.

> SARA/PENELOPE
> You are useful to me.  Isn't that
> enough?

> ODYSSEUS
> Perhaps once... but no more.

> SARA/PENELOPE
> What does that mean?  What you
> saying?  I'm no longer important to
> you?!

> ODYSSEUS
> I don't feel important.

> SARA/PENELOPE
> Of course you are.  I need you
> here.

> ODYSSEUS
> Because I'm useful.

> SARA/PENELOPE
> Because you're useful, yes.  You're
> needed.  You serve a purpose.

(CONTINUED)

                    ODYSSEUS
          I serve.

                    SARA/PENELOPE
          You serve me and all the people
          here.  We all rely on you.  We all
          need you.

                    ODYSSEUS
          Why?

                    SARA/PENELOPE
          What do you mean why?  That's what
          you do.  That's the way it
          is.  That's why you're here.

                    ODYSSEUS
          To serve.

                    SARA/PENELOPE
          Yes.

                    ODYSSEUS
          I am your servant.

                    SARA/PENELOPE
          Yes.

                    ODYSSEUS
          Forever.

                    SARA/PENELOPE
          For eternity.

ODYSSEUS jumps to his feet.

                    ODYSSEUS
          No!

                    SARA/PENELOPE
          Stop!

                    ODYSSEUS
          No, I'm not a slave.

                    SARA/PENELOPE
          You are.  A slave to your duty.

                    ODYSSEUS
          No more.

Darkness.  In darkness:

                    RACHEL/CALYPSO
You can leave her.

                    ODYSSEUS
I must.

SARA/PENELOPE is gone. Now it is RACHEL/CALYPSO, no longer
in her feathers but a flowing Greek gown which sparkles in
the light.

                    RACHEL/CALYPSO
But you're so tired... you need
rest.

                    ODYSSEUS
It gets so difficult...

                    RACHEL/CALYPSO
Of course.

                    ODYSSEUS
I do everything and yet it feels
like I do nothing.

                    RACHEL/CALYPSO
You feel trapped.

                    ODYSSEUS
I feel like I've lost my purpose.

                    RACHEL/CALYPSO
Perhaps you need a new purpose.

                    ODYSSEUS
I do... but I feel used up...
empty.

                    RACHEL/CALYPSO
There's more inside you... much
more... you're not empty... just
locked inside yourself... I have
the key.

                    ODYSSEUS
The key?  Key to what?

                    RACHEL/CALYPSO
Your desires.  Your purpose.

                    ODYSSEUS
You have the answer?

(CONTINUED)

                    RACHEL/CALYPSO
          I do... come... be with me... I
          will help you search inside
          yourself... help to find what
          you're seeking.

                    ODYSSEUS
          Can you do that for me?

                    RACHEL/CALYPSO
          I can do so much for you.  More
          than you dreamed of.

                    ODYSSEUS
          But at what price?

                    RACHEL/CALYPSO
          Do you not trust me?

                    ODYSSEUS
          I don't trust anyone.

                    RACHEL/CALYPSO
          You can trust me.

                    ODYSSEUS
          I want to...

                    RACHEL/CALYPSO
          I only want to help.

ODYSSEUS starts to go with her but stops.

                    ODYSSEUS
          Why?  Why do you want to help me?

                    RACHEL/CALYPSO
          I love you.

                    ODYSSEUS
          But what do you want in return?

                    RACHEL/CALYPSO
          Your eternal love.

                    ODYSSEUS
          I can't give you that.

                    RACHEL/CALYPSO
          But I will give you everything in
          my power... help you to find your
          purpose... with me.

                                        (CONTINUED)

> ODYSSEUS
> What if that's not my
> purpose?  What if I'm need
> elsewhere?  My home... my
> children... my people...

> RACHEL/CALYPSO
> Be with me...

> SARA/PENELOPE
> And be your slave.

> RACHEL/CALYPSO
> Only a slave to his passion...
> better than a hopeless servant.

> SARA/PENELOPE
> It's his purpose!

> RACHEL/CALYPSO
> It's only yours!

ODYSSEUS grabs his head in pain.

> ODYSSEUS
> Stop!  Stop this now! You're
> tearing me apart!

Darkness.  The sounds of the storm return.  Odysseus is tied
to the mast again.

> ODYSSEUS (CONT.)
> Love... passion... purpose...
> needs... they drive me mad yet I
> feel empty when they are gone... my
> chest is filled with hurt... I can
> hardly breathe... Why do I need
> what destroys me? (long pause) I'm
> so tired.  I've been on this
> journey and fought in this war and
> yet there are still no answers...
> still no end... I keep searching...
> keep looking... and keep finding
> the same emptiness... the same
> trap.  The same path which loops in
> on itself... infinity... the
> unending loop.  Why can't I break
> the cycle and find a way out?

END OF SCENE

* * * * * * * * * * *

PART 8

"DEMONS"

                    BLAKE
Don't get any closer.  I don't want
to hurt you.

I've been trying to hide them.  I
wanted to protect you.  I hid the
truth from you.  I wanted to keep
you safe.  But there's no place
where we can hide.

Look in to my eyes.  Can you see
them?  Can you see them looking out
at you?  Can you see the darkness
in me?  I want them out of me.  I
want to rip them out of my
soul.  But they cling to me.
Holding on so tight... so tight
that I can't breathe.

Can you show me how to get rid of
them?  Can you help me?

You're getting too close.  I don't
want them to hurt you.

Please don't hurt her too.  Please
leave her alone.  You have me...
you don't need her too.

See what you've done.  You've made
them angry.  They are punishing
me.  They always punish me.  They
want to punish you too.

I can't let you!  No!  But I have
to... it's the only way to make the
pain inside me go away.

Lift me up... I feel like I am
falling... I'm drowning
inside.  You feel so far away.  I
feel like nothing can reach
me.  I'm lost.  I'm so
weak.  Please... I can't take this
much longer.  I can't do this
anymore.  How can I live with this
pain inside me?

There's no place we can
hide.  We'll never escape them.

                    (MORE)

                         BLAKE (cont'd)
          Run!  Run before they find you!  I
          am hell bound. They are burned in
          my soul.  They are a part of me.
          But there is still hope for you.
          Hope... there's no hope anymore...
          I'm too far gone... buried...
          buried deep inside this tomb...
          lost and undone.  My kingdom has
          come, his will was done... I am
          beyond heaven and earth... there is
          no deliverance from this evil.
          Why are you still here?  Save
          yourself.  Please... you
          can't.  You're not strong enough.
          You can't stop them.

          You can never take them from me.

END OF SCENE

* * * * * * * * * * * *

PART 9


"GRACE"

INT. Dimly Lit Room. Night.

A noose hangs with a large shadow cast on the wall.  Cut to
a chair tumbling over.

                         GRACE (VOICE)
          Don't worry.  I'm here.

Cut to Jude in the arms of Grace.  Jude's eyes are closed
and Grace rocks him.

                         GRACE (CONT.)
          You'll be okay.

Jude's eyes pop open and he pulls away from Grace.  He can
see her now.  She is in white and looks at him
concerned.  He touches his neck and looks away.

                         GRACE (CONT.)
          Was it that bad?

                         JUDE
          What?

                                            (CONTINUED)

                         GRACE
             Your life?

Jude shakes his head and can't look at her.

                         JUDE
             Yes.

                         GRACE
             You couldn't see very well.  I
             tried to give you light, but you
             couldn't see.

                         JUDE
             I'm blind.

                         GRACE
             You only think you are.

                         JUDE
             And what would I see?  Pain?
             Suffering?

                         GRACE
             Love?

                         JUDE
             There's no love anymore.

                         GRACE
             That's not true.

Grace goes to touch Jude. He shudders but then falls in to
her arms.

                         JUDE
             You were too late.

                         GRACE
             No... I wasn't.

Jude falls asleep in her arms.  A woman in black comes from
the shadows from behind Grace.  She hisses when she talks.

                         BEZ
             What are you doing?

                         GRACE
             Helping him rest?

                         BEZ
             He's mine now.

                    GRACE
          No... not yet.

                    BEZ
          You had your chance.  You failed.

                    GRACE
          Not yet.

Grace gently places Jude on the ground asleep.  Bez grabs
Grace and pulls her away from him.

                    BEZ
          He's marked now.  He comes with me.

                    GRACE
          When he wakes, the mark will be
          gone.

                    BEZ
          I'm taking him now.

                    GRACE
          Touch him...

Grace wraps her arms around Bez like a friendly hug.

                    GRACE (CONT.)
          ...and I'll destroy you.

Bez fights free of Grace's embrace.

                    BEZ
          What are you doing?

                    GRACE
          I'm not finished with him.

                    BEZ
          But he's finished with you.  He
          made his choice.

                    GRACE
          It was the wrong choice.

                    BEZ
          Doesn't matter.  What's done is
          done.

                    GRACE
          And shall be undone.

Bez gets a happy, evil look on her face.

                    BEZ
          You'll be punished.

Grace bends down next to the sleeping Jude and touches his
hair lovingly.

                  GRACE
          I know.

                    BEZ
          A sacrifice.

Grace nods.

                  GRACE
          A sacrifice.

Bez laughs.

                    BEZ
          You idiot.  You'd give up
          everything for him?

                  GRACE
          Everything.

                    BEZ
          So be it.

Bez goes to the chair, grabs it and slams it upright to the
floor with a thunderous boom.

                  BEZ (CONT.)
          It's his choice though.

                  GRACE
          I know.

                  BEZ
          What if he doesn't love you?

Grace looks at him sadly.  He's starting to stir.  Bez bends
down next to them and reach for him.  Grace pushes her hand
away.

                  GRACE
         Don't touch him.

                  BEZ
         You don't know if he loves you, do
         you?

Bez laughs.

                                                    (CONTINUED)

                    BEZ (CONT.)
          You're such a fool.  See you on the
          other side.

Bez fades in to the darkness. Jude stirs. Grace helps up as
he wakes.

                    JUDE
          What have you done?

                    GRACE
          I saved you.

                    JUDE
          Why?

                    GRACE
          It wasn't right... you shouldn't
          have tried that.

                    JUDE
          That's not your choice.  It's mine.

Jude goes for the chair. Grace grabs him.

                    GRACE
          No!

                    JUDE
          Why are you stopping me?

                    GRACE
          I can't let you.

                    JUDE
          You said you'd fix things.  You
          said you'd make it better.

                    GRACE
          And I will.

                    JUDE
          When?  I want to know when...

Jude falls to his knees.

                    JUDE (CONT.)
          I can't do this much longer.  I'm
          slowly slipping away.

                    GRACE
          I won't let that happen.

                                        (CONTINUED)

                    JUDE
          Can you see what's happening to
          me?

                    GRACE
          I see everything.

                    JUDE
          Then you can see how it is all
          tearing me apart.  I'm in
          pieces.  It hurts so bad.

Bez watches from the darkness.  Grace sees her.

                    GRACE
          Go!  It's not over!

                    BEZ
          Soon.

Bez leaves again.

                    JUDE
          She was there again wasn't
          she?  She's always there.  Waiting.

                    GRACE
          I won't let her hurt you.

                    JUDE
          It's too late.

                    GRACE
          It's never too late.

                    JUDE
          Some things can't be fixed.  Some
          things need to be thrown away.

He moves away from her toward the chair but she clings to
him.

                    GRACE
          No!

                    JUDE
          Are you doing this for me or for
          yourself?

                    GRACE
          For both of us.

                         JUDE
              There is no us and I don't want
              there to be a me anymore.

Jude breaks away.  Darkness.

                         GRACE
              No!

Chair falls.  Silence a few moments then:

                         GRACE (VOICE)
              I've got you.  You'll be okay.

                         JUDE
              I'm so tired.

                         GRACE
              Rest.  I will watch over you.

Jude closes his eyes and rests in her arms.  Bez hisses from
the darkness.

                         BEZ
              You can't keep doing this.

                         GRACE
              I can. And I will... until I get it
              right.

                         BEZ
              You'll tear his soul apart!

Grace lays Jude down to rest.  She rises and faces Bez.

                         GRACE
              You've already done more damage
              than I can do.  I will find a way
              to heal him.

                         BEZ
              It's impossible.  Quit torturing
              him.  He's mine.

                         GRACE
              Torture?  This is nothing compared
              to what you have done.

                         BEZ
              Stop doing this.  It's useless.

(CONTINUED)

                         GRACE
               You're the one who should have
               stopped long ago.

                         BEZ
               And he's too far gone.

                         GRACE
               Not true.  I see hope.

                         BEZ
               He's not yours.  Quit this
               stupidity and give him to me.

                         GRACE
               No.  I'm not giving up on
               him.  Never.

                         BEZ
               Then it'll be like this for
               eternity.  This will be your Hell.

Bez points to long line of chairs that fade in to the
darkness.

                         BEZ (CONT.)
               This will how it will go.  He steps
               on to the chair...

Bez topples the first chair.

                         BEZ (CONT.)
               You save him.  But he goes back to
               the chair.

Bez topples the next chair.

                         BEZ (CONT.)
               You save him.  But he goes again.

Bez topples the next chair and then the next.

                         BEZ (CONT.)
               There's nothing you can do to
               change that.

Grace suddenly realizes something.  She stops Bez from
knocking over the next chair.

                         GRACE
               But you can change this.

>                    BEZ
>           What?

>                    GRACE
>           You're the answer.  You can change
>           things for him.  You did this to
>           him so you can undo it.

>                    BEZ
>           Why would I do that?

>                    GRACE
>           Because you loved him once.

Bez hisses at Grace.

>                    BEZ
>           You're wrong.

>                    GRACE
>           You don't love him
>           anymore.  Release him to me.

>                    BEZ
>           Never!

>                    GRACE
>           Why won't you give him to me?

>                    BEZ
>           He's mine!  He gave his soul to me
>           and he's mine!  He struck a
>           deal.  End of story.

>                    GRACE
>           And you demanded more than his soul
>           with the deal... and you fell in
>           love.

>                    BEZ
>           He loved me too.  He still
>           does.  Stupid man.  I'm killing him
>           but he keeps coming back to me.

>                    GRACE
>           Isn't that what love is?

>                    BEZ
>           Shut up!

>                    GRACE
>           Give him to me.

(CONTINUED)

                         BEZ
          Shut up!

                         GRACE
          I love him.  I can heal him.  Make
          him the way he used to be.

Bez pulls a large blade from her robes.

                         BEZ
          I've had enough of this.

Bez goes to Jude.

                         BEZ (CONT.)
          He's finished and so are you.

Bez raises the blade and Grace closes her eyes.  Bez holds
the blade above her head ready to strike at Jude.  She
can't.  She turns to Grace and moves as if to strike her
down.  She can't.  She throws down the blade.

                         BEZ (CONT.)
          Take him.  Take him and go.  Now!

Grace rushes to Jude, quickly wakes him.  She gets him to
leave with her and he goes still not sure what is
happening.  Bez goes to the next chair still upright.  We
see the shadow of the noose.  The lights fade to black and
then there is the crash of the chair.  After a few moments
of silence:

                         GRACE (VOICE)
          Don't worry.  I'm here.

END OF SCENE

* * * * * * * * * * *

PART 10


"BREAKING HEART"

                         JO
          You want to break up... sure... no
          problem... yeah, I wanted to break
          up too.  I've been thinking about
          it from the day we met.  This is a
          person I will need to break up
          with.  But hey... you beat me to
          it.  No hard feelings.
                         (MORE)

                                                      (CONTINUED)

                              JO (cont'd)

(shrugs and turns away)

Be friends?

(turns with a huge smile)

Sure!  I'd love to be
friends.  That's the natural
evolution of most
relationships.  Have a fling and
then boom... friends.  I'm sure
some of the best friendships
started that way.

(overly enthusiastic)

I look forward to hanging out with
you, buddy.  Let's meet up and go
to...

([insert stereotypical place
opposite gender likes to hang out:
Hooters, Victoria's Secret,
football game, shopping, etc.])

...some time and hang out.

(yells)

That would be GREAT!

(quiet/angry/eyes closed)

What?  Upset?  No, I'm not
upset.  Why would I be... upset...

(starts to cry)

No, I'm not crying.  I said, I'm
not crying!

(bursts in to tears)

I don't want your pity.  I don't
want a shoulder to cry on.  I
want... to be left...

(yells)

...ALONE!  Don't you get it.  I
want to be alone!
                    (MORE)

                                        (CONTINUED)

                         JO (cont'd)

(pauses... sadly reflects)

I've always wanted to be alone.  I
never wanted to get close to
anyone.  I never wanted us to get
close.  And I guess I was closer to
you than you were to me.

(turns angry)

Don't lie to me.  I know you don't
mean it.  I don't want to hear any
more lies!  I don't want you to
make something up so you can get
out of this.  I want it all laid
out on the table.

(yells)

I want to know the truth!

(long pause... cries... then
manages to say)

I want to know why you are breaking
my heart.

END OF SCENE

* * * * * * * * * *

PART 11


"FALLING AWAY FROM YOU"

Mel is alone in a busy street.  There are sounds of crowds
of people.  There are cars honking.  Mel wants to cross the
street but cars and rushing by.  He acts like invisible
people are pushing him.  He gets in a panic.  May appears
and the noises stop.  Mel sees her and runs to her.  She
wants to hug him but can't because of some invisible
barrier.

                         MEL
              Every time I fly, I wonder why I'm
              flying.  Especially when I'm flying
              alone.  What's the point of going
              if I leave you behind?  What if
              you're not there when I get back?

                    MAY
Do you really worry about that?

                    MEL
I worry about everything.

                    MAY
Why now?  I thought you were
better.

                    MEL
I am.  I was.  Most of the time...

                    MAY
Are you okay?

                    MEL
Not really.

                    MAY
Is it that hard for you?

                    MEL
Everything is hard for me... well,
it was... you make it easier... I
thought I would be okay on my
own... but you're my anchor.  You
keep me steady.

                    MAY
I want to.  Is it that hard without
me?

                    MEL
I feel like I'm in a fog.  Slightly
out of sync.  I'm here, on this
crowded street but I don't really
see anyone.  They don't see me
either.

                    MAY
I see you.

                    MEL
You always do.

                    MAY
I see so much more than you see
yourself.

                    MEL
I want to be that person you
see.  I really do...

(CONTINUED)

                         MAY
             Then be that person.

                         MEL
             I'm scared.

                         MAY
             Of what?

                         MEL
             I don't know.  Everything.  The
             world scares me.

Sirens.

                         MEL (CONT.)
             What is that?

                         MAY
             What do you hear?

                         MEL
             Sirens?  Strange sirens.

Sirens mix with cries.

                         MEL (CONT.)
             Strange sounds.  Echoing through
             the city.  The empty city.  It like
             I don't see anyone but I know there
             are there.  I feel crowded but
             alone.

                         MAY
             I'm here, Mel.  You don't have to
             be afraid.

The sirens stop.

                         MEL
             How can you be here?  We said
             good-bye.  I hate saying
             good-bye.  Those tears... those
             tears in your beautiful eyes.

                         MAY
             Those tears are because I love
             you.  I don't cry for anyone
             else.  Tears aren't always bad... I
             cried when we first made love.

                    MEL
          You did.  I was worried I'd hurt
          you.

                    MAY
          No, never.  It was so nice... I
          cried.

                    MEL
          Tears...

                    MAY
          Tears of love.

                    MEL
          Have there been too many
          tears?  Have you cried too much?

                    MAY
          I love the way you touch me
          inside.  I was frozen once.  The
          ice queen.  No one could
          penetrate.  But you did... somehow
          you did...

                    MEL
          And now you have so much love... so
          much wonderful love to give.

                    MAY
          Do I give you enough?

                    MEL
          So much and more.  It's such a
          wonderful feeling... to really be
          loved.  I mean, people always say
          "I love you" but what does it
          mean?  There's so much more to it.

                    MAY
          Is that our love?

                    MEL
          It is.

                    MAY
          Come home and I will give you love.

                    MEL
          I want that love... so badly.  I
          never want to leave that love
          again.

Sirens again.

                    MEL (CONT.)
          What is that?  What is going
          on?  Is someone hurt?

                    MAY
          I don't hear them.

                    MEL
          They're getting closer.

                    MAY
          You'll be okay.

                    MEL
          I want to be with you.

Sirens echo in the city... mix with ghostly cries.

                    MEL (CONT.)
          I'm so scared.  I wish I knew where
          they were going.

                    MAY
          No where... they're going no where.

                    MEL
          That's how I feel... no where...
          going no where... without you it's
          no where.

                    MAY
          I felt that way before us.

Sirens/cries fade.

                    MEL
          I love being a part of you.

                    MAY
          Like two halves...

                    MEL
          ...that become one.  You were made
          for me.  I really believe you were
          made for me.

                    MAY
          I am yours.

                    MEL
          A gift from above... now that's
          worth flying for... to reach up
          high enough to catch you... A
          spirit in the clouds... my angel.

(CONTINUED)

                         MAY
              You're so sweet to me.

                         MEL
              I hope so.  You mean so much to
              me.

                         MAY
              I better go now.  Are you going to
              be okay?

                         MEL
              I think so.  It helps to see you...
              to hear you.

                         MAY
              Is it enough?

                         MEL
              I never get enough.  The world is
              too demanding.

The sirens again.

                         MAY
              Don't let anything get in the way
              of us.

                         MEL
              The world is screaming at me.  I
              don't want to listen anymore.

The sirens cry.

                         MAY
              Then don't listen.  Shut it
              out.  Listen to my voice.  Listen
              to my words... I love you.

The sounds stop again.

                         MEL
              Such sweet words.  I love you.

                         MAY
              When you say them... yes.

                         MEL
              I miss you... so bad.

May looks sad.  Sirens start and lights flash red as they
get closer.  Mel looks at the lights and May tries to reach
for him but can't.  She cries and leaves.

                                                    (CONTINUED)

> MEL (CONT.)
> I always think I want to go
> somewhere but I am always sorry
> when I do.  I thought I had to take
> a journey to find happiness, when
> in reality, happiness is at home
> with you.  I guess the journeys
> make me appreciate you more.  I
> journeyed so far, but the best
> thing was right at my door.  Who
> would have thought that the best
> thing in the universe was only a
> walk away... no flying... no great
> voyage... just turn around and
> look... and ...  (sees she is gone)
> That's something good, right?  Just
> trying to find some good because I
> don't feel so good now.

Sirens mix with cries.

> MEL (CONT.)
> Alone.  I hate being alone.   The
> plane lifts me up but I feel like I
> am falling.  (He falls to his
> knees)  Falling away from you.

He falls to the ground in a heap.  There are sirens, red
flashing lights, cries for help.

END OF SCENE

* * * * * * * * * *

PART 12

"DUMMY"

> DJ
> This is not me.

(Points to self.)
> This is me over here.

(Points to dummy)
> He can't say the right thing so I
> have to speak for him. You know
> those people who always say the
> wrong thing at the worst moment in
> the worst possible way? Well that's
> me... Well, him... Us... We. Not
> the royal we either.

(Turns to dummy like he said something)
Babbling? Yes... Thanks dummy... I
will get to the point.

I didn't mean to stop talking to
you... I didn't mean to turn in to
him over there... But I just wanted
to stop ... Stop before I did any
more damage. It feels like my words
cause so much destruction. It's
like a flower in the wind. You love
the gentle breeze of my words when
I say sweet things to you... You
open up yourself and bloom for me
in my kindest moments. But the
harsh words break you and tear you
apart like a storm. My words storm
and rage over you like some black
cloud raining over us ripping the
gentle petals from you. Like a
flower caught in a tornado.

I want to whisper sweet things
again. I want to nourish you and
help you grow your beautiful
blossom again, but I get so scared
... I become so afraid of what I
will do. You deserve kindness...
Upon deserve beauty. You deserve
loving words. I want that too. But
I feel silenced. I feel crippled
inside. I feel broken.

There are so many things I want to
say to you though. So many
wonderful things I feel for you...
See in you... Get from you.

I feel better because of you. Like
you healed me in some way. I felt
sick emotionally before I had you
in my life. I felt spiritually
dead. You brought me back to life,
resurrected the spirit inside me,
healed me. You're my angel. That's
what you are to me. An angel. So
delicate. Such a pure spirit. No
hardness hiding the goodness and
purity. You leave yourself open to
me, giving your full self to me,
hiding nothing. You give everything
to me... And keep nothing for
yourself. You give me your wings so
                    (MORE)

>                         DJ (cont'd)
>           I can fly. You'd remove your heart
>           just to keep mine beating.
>
>           You are the greatest gift that has
>           ever been given to me. You complete
>           me. You make me whole.
>
>           I wish I could speak those words to
>           you.
>
> (Looks at dummy)
>           I wish this dummy could say what I
>           feel.

END OF SCENE

* * * * * * * * * *

PART 13


"THE FOOD OF LOVE"

A professor MULIGAN rushes around a theatre trying to get
ready for his class.  He plays some instrumental music to
try and calm himself.  He adjusts his podium, strikes a pose
and then gets nervous and adjusts the podium again.  He
bumps in to his easel which has Shakespeare visuals on
it.  He fixes the visuals, looks at his watch and then
rushes back to the podium.  He realizes his folder is empty
and rushes to his briefcase.  He pulls out a folder thick
with notes.  He stands and JULIE walks up behind him.

>                         JULIE
>           Hello professor.

MULIGAN drops all his papers.  Julie tries to supress a
laugh.  She smiles at him kindly as he stands there looking
sadly at the pile.

>                         MULIGAN
>           Hello Julie.

Julie starts gathering papers.

>                         JULIE
>           Here, let me help you.

Muligan slowly bends down to help her.

                         MULIGAN
          I'd be upset about them being out
          of order but they weren't in order
          anyway.  I dropped them on the way
          here.

                         JULIE
          Oh dear.

                         MULIGAN
          I'm so nervous about this lecture.

                         JULIE
          Then why are you giving it?

                         MULIGAN
          Good question.

                         JULIE
          You're always doing stuff like this
          but you don't seem to enjoy it that
          much.

                         MULIGAN
          And yet you come to every one.

                         JULIE
          I enjoy it.

                         MULIGAN
          You do?

                         JULIE
          Yeah.

                         MULIGAN
          Thank you.

                         JULIE
          For what?

                         MULIGAN
          It's nice to hear someone likes it.

                         JULIE
          I'm sure lots of people do.

                         MULIGAN
          But it's nice to hear someone say
          it.  And even better if they
          remember something from it.

                         JULIE
          Like the true identity of William
          Shakespeare... Edward de Vere.

                         MULIGAN
          Wow, you do really listen.  I mean
          I don't say that he's Edward
          conclusively, but...

Muligan is all excited but starts dropping his papers
again.  Julie stops him by taking his hands in hers.  He
stops at her touch and looks her in the eyes.

                         JULIE
          I know... I've listened.

                         MULIGAN
          You really have.  What's your
          favorite lecture?

                         JULIE
          Romeo and Juliet of course.

                         MULIGAN
          Two star crossed lovers.

                         JULIE
          From totally different places...
          totally different lives... yet
          drawn together despite their
          differences.

                         MULIGAN
          Those stories have stood the test
          of time.  That's amazing
          literature... living literature
          that never dies.

                         JULIE
          I love your passion.  That's why I
          come so often.  I can feel your
          excitement.

Muligan feels some different excitement looking at her and
hearing the compliments.  He turns and takes his papers to
the podium.

                         MULIGAN
          Thank you.

Julie ducks under his arms between him and the podium.

                                                    (CONTINUED)

                         JULIE
          Want me to organize these for
          you?  I bet I could.

Muligan sniffs her hair but then is shocked at himself and
moves away.

                         MULIGAN
          Um... sounds like a fun
          challenge.  Is is like Twelth's
          Night?  Trying to reunite the twins
          lost at sea.

                         JULIE
          Or is it like the Tempest... lost
          in a storm and shipwrecked... on a
          podium?

Muligan holds up a piece of paper.

                         MULIGAN
          Gentle breath of your my sails;
          Must fill, or else my project fails

Julie blows on his paper and his flies out of his
hands.  They look at each other a moment and smile.  Julie
picks up another paper and blows it away.

                         JULIE
          "Blow, blow, thou winter wind; Thou
          are not so unkind as man's
          ingratitude."

                         MULIGAN
          As You Like It.  Man's
          ingratitute... I get plenty of that
          here at the university. "Most
          friendship is feigning, most loving
          is folly."  Do you believe that?

                         JULIE
          Not in the least.  Shakespeare says
          many things.  But we can't believe
          in Shakespeare.  Only each other.

                         MULIGAN
          Not God?

                         JULIE
          God wrote the play... we're the
          actors.

(CONTINUED)

                    MULIGAN
          "All the World's a Stage. And all
          the men and women merely players."

                    JULIE
          Exactly.

                    MULIGAN
          Or did Shakepeare believe men were
          gods?  "What a piece of work is a
          man, how noble in reason, how
          infinite in faculties, in form and
          moving how express and admirable,
          in action how like an angel, in
          apprehension how like a god."

                    JULIE
          Hamlet was crazy... "Now, God be
          praised, that to believing souls
          gives light in darkness, comfort in
          despair."

                    MULIGAN
          Is Henry the Sixth a more reliable
          source than Hamlet?

                    JULIE
          Henry was a real person.

                    MULIGAN
          True... wow, you really have
          learned a lot about Shakespeare.

                    JULIE
          I think a lot of people know about
          the King Henries.

                    MULIGAN
          The quotes... the insight... I'm
          impressed.

                    JULIE
          I learned it all from you.

                    MULIGAN
          But no one else seems to have
          learned that much... I seem to be
          speaking in to the wind.  It is a
          tale told by an idiot. "Full of
          sound and fury. Signifying
          nothing."

                                        (CONTINUED)

                         JULIE
              That's MacBeth. Not you.

                         MULIGAN
              That's what it seems like
              though.  Nothing gets through.

                         JULIE
              It does to me.  Is that enough?

                         MULIGAN
              Maybe it is.

Muligan looks at Julie a long moment and she smiles back.

                         MULIGAN (CONT.)
              "Speak low..."

                         JULIE
              You got me there... don't recognize
              the quote.

                         MULIGAN
              "Excellent wretch..."

                         JULIE
              You're studdering in Shakespeare.

                         MULIGAN
              When does my lecture begin?

                         JULIE
              Not for an hour.

                         MULIGAN
              I'm not ready.

                         JULIE
              Then cancel it.

                         MULIGAN
              I can't.

                         JULIE
              Why not?

                         MULIGAN
              The university...

                         JULIE
              Who cares...

She takes his face in her hands.

                              JULIE (CONT.)
          What do you want?

He looks at her longingly and there is a long pause.

                              MULIGAN
          Happiness.

Julie goes to the podium.

                              JULIE
          Does this make you happy?

                              MULIGAN
          It used to... but no so much
          anymore.

                              JULIE
          Then find something that does.

                              MULIGAN
          Oh happy dagger...

                              JULIE
          I think Juliet was being ironic
          when she said that.

                              MULIGAN
          Joy... that's what I need... some
          joy... "Joy, gentle friends, joy
          and fresh days of love..."

                              JULIE
          Joy... and love.

                              MULIGAN
          "A heart to love, and in that
          heart, Courage, to make's love
          known."

                              JULIE
          MacBeth.  Do you have the courage?

                              MULIGAN
          I don't know if I do.

                              JULIE
          "I know no ways to mince it in
          love, but directly to say 'I love
          you'"

                         MULIGAN
          Henry the Fifth. "You have
          witchcraft in your lips."

                         JULIE
          Okay... bad choice... how about "I
          humbly do beseech of your pardon,
          For too much loving you"

                         MULIGAN
          Othello doesn't end well either.

                         JULIE
          I need a quote from a comedy.

                         MULIGAN
          Nobody quotes the comedies...

                         JULIE
          But you did... "Speak low if you
          speak love."

                         MULIGAN
          You pretended you didn't know.

                         JULIE
          You've used that quote a few
          times... I finally remembered it.

                         MULIGAN
          So much for being subtile.

                         JULIE
          Why be subtile?

                         MULIGAN
          Should we be doing this?

                         JULIE
          Shouldn't you be happy?

                         MULIGAN
          Can I be happy?

                         JULIE
          You can.

                         MULIGAN
          I don't know how.

                         JULIE
          Then let me teach you.

                         MULIGAN
               How?

She takes his hands and moves close to him and strokes his
hand.

                         JULIE
               With a kiss.

                         MULIGAN
               "O, then, dear saint, let lips do
               what hands do."

Lights fade to black except for a light on the easel with
the quote "If music be the food of love, play on".  Music
plays louder.

END OF SCENE

* * * * * * * * * *

PART 14


"BEFORE YOU PUNCH ME"

                         MELVIN
               Before you punch me there is
               something you should know.

               This woman we're fighting over is
               no ordinary woman... You don't know
               how good you had it.

               If I am going to die I want the
               world to know how great she is...
               Why do you want me to shut up? You
               afraid? You afraid I will say
               something that will hurt you?  You
               that sensitive? You gonna cry,
               Softy?

               Then listen... Punch me all you
               want when I am done... Beat me to a
               pulp but let me say how I feel...
               For her.. Do this one kindness for
               her... She's worth it.

               Do you know about
               serendipity?  Word too big for
               you?  I should stick to one or two
               syllables when speaking to you...
                         (MORE)

MELVIN (cont'd)

"Serendipity means a "happy
accident" or "pleasant surprise"; a
fortunate mistake. Specifically,
the accident of finding something
good while not specifically
searching for it."

That's what our love was... A happy
accident.  We didn't plan on this.

She is amazing ... She is so very
good... She has made me happier
than I thought was
possible.  Before her, it was like
I was living in black and white and
suddenly she brought color to my
world.

And by some miracles she chose
me.  I thought she was wonderful of
course but I never thought in a
million years she'd want me.  She
was the princess to my pauper.  The
batman to my robin.  The Picard to
my Wesley Crusher.  She was so much
better and I was so unworthy yet
she wants me.  By some incredible
stoke of luck, she wants me.  And
her kisses will last me until
death... Which might not be very
far off.

Yes, we're talking about the same
woman, you idiot.

(Takes off glasses)

And now you can punch me.

END OF SCENE

* * * * * * * * * *

PART 15

"HEART ATTACK"

People are on a subway.  A woman (Dana) is standing
listening to music.  Gus is sitting looking at his watch
impatiently.  Jay is next to him with a magazine.  Lissy
sits a ways away reading a book.

                    GUS
          How long have we been stuck
          here?  I don't think we've moved at
          all in an hour.  I can't sit here
          all day. Uh... this is driving me
          nuts.  What's the hold up?


                    JAY
          No clue.  Did you see this article
          about peace negotiations in North
          Korea?  Kim Jong Un says he'll only
          talk to Angelina Jolie.  Somebody
          wants a spanking.

                    GUS
          What? Oh, man.


Dana looks over at Gus and notices he is in distress.

                    JAY
          I made that last part up.  It
          doesn't say that.


                    GUS
          Man... oh...

                    JAY
          You okay?

                    GUS
          I... uh... man...

                    JAY
          You don't look so good.

                    GUS
          What's wrong with me?

                    JAY
          Maybe it's something you ate.  That
          egg salad sandwich was not a
          natural color.

                    GUS
          Man... Uh!  I think this is it...
          this is that heart attack my doctor
                    (MORE)


                                        (CONTINUED)

                         GUS (cont'd)
          promised me... I think this is the
          big one...

                         JAY
          Geez... really?  Now?  Can't you
          hold it in or something?

                         GUS
          Oh... oh... man!

Suddenly Dana goes over to Gus, sits next to him and gives
him a huge kiss.  He is startled at first and then calms
down and enjoys it.  She stops kissing and Gus looks very
happy.

                         DANA
          There.  Better?

                         GUS
          All better.

                         DANA
          Good.

Dana goes back to her spot and listen to her music
again.  Gus and Jay look at her in amazement.

                         JAY
          What was that all about?

                         LISSY
          You were probably just having a
          panic attack.  She snapped you out
          of it.

                         GUS
          I'll say.

                         JAY
          Panic again... let's see what she
          does.

Dana smirks but doesn't look at them.

                         GUS
          Thank you.

Dana shrugs.

                         JAY
          She's hot too.  Ask her out.

                         GUS
          What?

                         JAY
          She's hot and she kissed you.  Ask
          her out.

                         GUS
          But... I... I'm so confused.

                         JAY
          The kiss was that good huh?

                         GUS
          Better than good.  That was the
          best kiss I've had in my whole
          life.

Dana smiles to herself and does something flirty with her
hair.

                         JAY
          She's flirting.  Go for it.

                         GUS
          Uh... uh...

                         JAY
          That's good. Panic.  She likes
          that.

                         GUS
          Stop.

                         JAY
          No, you stop.  Stop being so
          shy.  Stop missing out on
          life.  Stop hiding.  Life walked up
          to you and kissed you on the
          lips.  Give life a chance.  Quit
          being so dead all the time.

                         GUS
          I have been, haven't I?  Dead...
          dead for a long time.  I can't
          remember the last time I felt
          alive.

                         JAY
          I've known you a long time and I
          can't remember either.

                              GUS
                    What happened to me?

                              JAY
                    That's the problem.  Nothing
                    happened.  You never take a
                    chance.  You never take a
                    risk.  You play it safe and nothing
                    happens to you.

                              GUS
                    Until now.

                              JAY
                    Until now.  And now looks pretty
                    good from where I'm sitting.

Dana gives Jay a dirty look.

                              JAY (CONT.)
                    She's a firecracker.  Go talk to
                    her.

                              GUS
                    But what if... I mean if she...

                              JAY
                    She kissed you idiot.  She likes
                    you.  Go before I kick you in the
                    balls.

                              GUS
                    What?

                              JAY
                    I will hurt you if you don't go
                    talk to her.

                              GUS
                    Fine.  Geez.

Gus goes shyly over to Dana.  He isn't sure what to say.

                              DANA
                    Hi.  I'm Dana.

                              GUS
                    Hi.  I'm the guy you kissed... Gus.

                              DANA
                    That's a cute name.

                              GUS
                    Really?

                              DANA
                    Adorable.

                              GUS
                    It's short for Angus.

                              DANA
                    Even cuter.

                              GUS
                    So... uh... why... uh...

                              DANA
                    Why did I kiss you?

Gus laughs.

                              GUS
                    Yes.

                              DANA
                    Believe it or not, we ride this
                    subway a lot together.  I watch
                    you... because there's something
                    about you that's different from
                    everyone... a sweetness about
                    you.  You always give up your seat
                    for women.  You even did for me
                    once.  If someone forgets a coat or
                    a bag, you get it and chase after
                    them.  If a woman is being bugged
                    by some creepy guy and they don't
                    like it, you'll interrupt and make
                    sure the woman safely gets to a
                    taxi, even if the woman doesn't
                    know you're doing it.

                              GUS
                    You saw all that.

                              DANA
                    Yup... I'm a stalker.

Gus laughs.

                              GUS
                    A good one too.  I never noticed.

                                                      (CONTINUED)

                              DANA
                    I'm a ninja.

                              GUS
                    Ninja stalker.  Good combination.

                              DANA
                    Thanks.

                              GUS
                    So that's why you kissed me?

                              DANA
                    Well, in a way.  But even though
                    you do all these nice, sweet
                    things, you always look so stressed
                    and unhappy.  You look like you're
                    about to have a heart attack at any
                    moment.  I see the panic in your
                    eyes sometimes.  I see the stress
                    overwhelming you.

                              GUS
                    I didn't think anyone noticed.

                              DANA
                    Not even your friend it appears.

Jay is checking out Lissy.

                              GUS
                    He has other things on his mind.

                              DANA
                    So I told myself, next time you
                    looked stressed and overwhelmed and
                    on the edge of a heart attack, I
                    was going to give you a great big
                    kiss.

                              GUS
                    That's crazy... and so very nice at
                    the same time.

                              DANA
                    Did you like it?

                              GUS
                    I really liked it.  It might be the
                    nicest thing that's ever happened
                    to me.

                    DANA
          Really?  That's the sweetest thing
          anyone has ever said to me.

Dana gives Gus another huge kiss.

                    GUS
          Wow.

                    DANA
          Wow worthy kiss... I didn't think I
          was that good.

                    GUS
          You are.

                    DANA
          I really enjoy kissing you.  I had
          a feeling I would.

                    GUS
          I'm so glad you kissed me.

                    DANA
          I'm so glad you liked it.

                    GUS
          The next car looks empty.  Want to
          go over there.

                    DANA
          And do what?

                    GUS
          Uh... well... I just... we can...
          talk.

                    DANA
          Okay.

Dana takes Gus by the hand and they exit to the next
car.  Jay goes over to Lissy.

                    JAY
          That was pretty wild huh?  Her
          kissing him like that.

                    LISSY
          I thought maybe she was giving a
          free sample or something.

                                              (CONTINUED)

                    JAY
You think she's "working"?

                    LISSY
No, I think she is for real.  I
believe her story.  I've noticed
him too.  He is a pretty neat
guy.  He deserves to find someone
who really appreciates him for who
he is.  I think we all noticed him
but she was the only one willing to
say anything.  Women usually don't
make the first move.  And he's a
sweet guy so he wouldn't make his
move.  So he was alone... until
now.  And now he looks so
happy.  That... what happened
there... was way better than this
book.  Trashy romances novels try
to give us the perfect fantasy but
that moment there was way better
because it was so much more
real.  Give me five minutes of
seeing that over reading hours of
this junk.

                    JAY
So women usually don't make the
first move huh?  They want to be
pursued, don't they?

                    LISSY
Out of everything I just said,
that's all you got out of it.

                    JAY
Pretty much... so what do you say?

                    LISSY
Oh, why not.

Lissy kisses Jay.  They end the kiss and look disappointed.

                    LISSY (CONT.)
I've had better.

                    JAY
Me too.

Jay goes back to his magazine and starts reading
again.  Lissy returns to her novel.

END OF SCENE

* * * * * * * * * *

PART 16


"PEARLS OF WISDOM"

(A young Idaho woman standing and staring with excited
fascination. A crib is near a chair behind her. Phrases in
quotes are done in voices of herself as younger or as other
characters in her life)

                         TYRANNY
              "Oh, my heck!" was all I could say
              when I first saw him. I'd never
              seen a man in quite this way
              before. I'd finally ripened... got
              my buds and flowered. Boys no
              longer caught my fancy; I was after
              a whole hunk of man now. I examined
              him with a horrific fascination
              that my mother had warned me about.
              The church too for that matter.

              (Mimicking an old lady)

              "Protect your pearls, girls," said
              Sister Sue as she handed us each a
              little baggy. The baggy held
              something like a clamshell. Inside
              each shell was a little pearl.

              (Pretending to be another young
              girl)

              "I wonder if it's real," Jennie
              Lynn asked wide eyed. I looked at
              my own pearl dipped in Elmer's
              glue.

              (Speaking as her younger self)

              "Not sure," I said as I studied it.
              "I think you bite it or something
              to tell. Saw this murder mystery on
              TV once. They'd made some kind of
              drug look like pearls. They crushed
              the pearl necklace with a tea cup
              and discovered it." Jennie Lynn
              just gave me a snot nosed upturned
              look.

                         (MORE)

                    TYRANNY (cont'd)
(Pause. Reflects as her older self)
The meaning of the pearl escaped me
until now.

(Mimicking old lady again)

"Keep that pearl safe. Don't let
the boys have your pearl until
you're ready," Sister Sue warned.
I'm sure she attached some
additional meaning to it, like
about marriage, but I couldn't
quite remember that part. I'd
forgotten most the lessons I'd
learned in church. Jesus no longer
man enough to keep my attention.

(Remembering. Looking longingly
ahead)

It was a cowboy that first got my
attention. As I stared at this man,
I grew hot and anxious. I about
threw him my pearl. "Take it, take
it, take it!" I chanted in my head.
He was nearly close enough to
taste. His horse sweaty from a long
ride, he stroked it gently. I
watched, wishing to be stroked.
Then he saw me, his eyes dancing,
his half grin giving me shivers.

(Mimicking a Western guy)

"Well, if it ain't my little cousin
Tyranny."

(Aside)

Mama had given me that name.
Grannie said momma lay there all
puzzled to high heaven about what
she was gonna call me.

(Mimicking her mom)

"Get me a dictionary," she ordered
and thumbed through Webster's til
she found a word that sounded nice:
Tyranny. She thought it was pretty
sounding.

                    (MORE)

                                           (CONTINUED)

                    TYRANNY (cont'd)
(Pause)

Now where was I? Oh, yeah, my
cousin Skeeter.

(Becoming her younger self)

"Hi, Skeeter," I climbed up the
side of a stall and straddled it.
Skeeter sauntered up and swatted me
on the backside.

(Smacks her own rear for effect,
then talks like a Western guy)

"Turning out to be a fine filly,
ain't ya?" I blushed, still felt
his hand where it had smacked me. I
liked it. I wanted him to do it
again. Skeeter leaned in close, so
close I could have kissed him. His
breath like beer and garlic mixed.
I could nearly taste it on my lips
as I licked them. "You better hold
on tight to your pearl or some
guy's gonna snatch it away." He
smacked my rear again and headed
out. I grinned uncontrollably.
Please, God, let Skeeter take my
pearl.

(Back to older self)

But he never did, though I wish he
had. At least my family might still
love me then. Then I'd be the
victim. This way, I am the bad one.
Raped at thirteen by a cousin would
have been far more noble in my
family's eyes. Sure Skeeter would
have been in for it, but at least
I'd be okay. You might be thinking
that I'm kind of strange thinking
that way about my cousin but I know
my history. People's been doing
this sort of thing for years you
know. Look at Egypt. All kinds of
those guys married family. In my
biology class they talked about
royalty marrying family like crazy
in England. Though I guess that was
kind of bad cause they got this
                 (MORE)

> TYRANNY (cont'd)
>
> disease. What was it again? Cycle cell ameba? Round here they still think family is okay. Plenty of people find love with a second or third cousin. Sometimes closer. Guys joke that they go to family reunions to meet girls. Mostly they don't, sometimes they do. My cousin Brock has it bad. His parents are related somehow and that's why Brock has fingers for toes and thumbs for fingers. Funniest looking hands you ever saw. We always point at Brock and say, now that's what happens when cousins marry. This ain't nearly as bad as the Eggerstons, distant cousins from a little town in Idaho called Mud Lake. Not too many people there that's not related. Old papa Eggerston has been married a few times. He's proud that his current wife isn't a blood relative; she's just his step-daughter. But previous family encounters had given his family strange hands without fingernails. Bizarre looking worms of hands. I'm like you all and I decided to stay clear of family. I shouldn't have bothered though. I'm worse off now because of it.
>
> (Pause. Goes to crib)
>
> I'd met Buck at a party. I got drunk. Drunk on beer and garlic. I must have eaten ten pizzas that night. Must have had twenty beers. Buck raped me... excuse me... courted me. They don't have date rape in these parts. Here they call it courtship.
>
> (Mimics mother)
>
> Sure, momma was a bit annoyed with old Buck. "You don't sleep with sixteen year old girls. You're thirty-one for Christ's sake." Momma gave him two options, marriage or jail. He took the
>
>                    (MORE)

                         TYRANNY (cont'd)
          logical course for once in his life
          and then slipped away.

          (Picks up baby from crib)

          So here I am, married, with a kid,
          still with my momma. My husband is
          somewhere getting some other girl
          drunk, taking her pearl. One day he
          may come back. But if he does, God
          help his pearls, cause I'm gonna
          cut 'em off. Cut 'em off and mount
          them like a couple of fish. Hang
          'em right next to my team roping
          trophies and label them "pearls of
          wisdom." They'll be a warning to
          any man who tries to take my girl's
          pearl.

          (Strokes babies head)

          I often sit here praying all men
          will die before my baby's old
          enough. My best hope for her is to
          be a lesbian. "Don't let them take
          your pearl, little Ennui." Then I
          sing to her, singing, hoping she'll
          remember...

          (Sings)

          "Hush little baby, don't say a
          word, Momma's gonna buy you a
          butcher knife. If that butcher
          knife won't cut, Momma's gonna
          hit'm with a pickup truck..."

END OF SCENE

* * * * * * * * * *

PART 17


"THE LAST CAN"

                         MYLA
          What's wrong, luv?

                         RIM
               I'm hungry.

RIM is staring at a can.

                         MYLA
               Then eat.  I don't mind.

                         RIM
               But it's the last one.

                         MYLA
               It's okay.

                         RIM
               What about you?  Aren't you hungry?

                         MYLA
               Not really.

He stares at it a long time.

                         RIM
               I can't believe it's the last one.

                         MYLA
               It had to happen sooner or later.

                         RIM
               I was hoping for much later.

He's looking for a can opener.

                         MYLA
               Check under the table.  Maybe it
               fell down there.

While Rim is under the table, Myla rushes over and grabs the
can and goes back to her chair, hiding the can.  Rim gets up
excited.

                         RIM
               Found it!  Time to eat... sure you
               don't want...

Rim stops when he sees the can is missing.

                         RIM (CONT.)
               What is this!  The hunger games!

Rim sits on the sofa and looks at the empty coffee table.

> RIM (CONT.)
> Was I just imagining there was a
> can there?  I am that hungry.

Myla has a playful voice.

> MYLA
> Maybe.

> RIM
> Or maybe someone took it.

Rim leaps up suddenly and starts tickling Myla.

> MYLA
> Stop, stop, you'll make me have to
> pee.

> RIM
> Hand it over!

> MYLA
> Okay, okay.

Myla holds up the can still laughing.  Rim takes the can.

> RIM
> You sure you don't want any.

> MYLA
> Nope.

Rim opens the can and keeps his eyes on her.  She is still
giggling a bit.  He has the can open but has no forks.  He
gets up to get a fork.  Myla moves forward a bit.

> RIM
> Don't you dare.  You'll make a
> mess.

Myla laughs.  Rim gets two forks and sits.  Myla goes and
sits by him.  He feeds her a bite and she returns the favor.

> MYLA
> The last can.

> RIM
> Afraid so.

> MYLA
> Or maybe it is the first meal
> before the feast.

(CONTINUED)

                    RIM
          The feast?

They are still feeding each other.

                    MYLA
          The feast that's waiting outside.

                    RIM
          Maybe the radiation fried up all
          the critters and turned them to
          jerky?

                    MYLA
          Too bad you're a vegetarian.

                    RIM
          And all the fruit is all dried up
          and ready for consumption.

                    MYLA
          And the water sparkles and bubbles
          like Perrier.

                    RIM
          But you don't like Perrier.

                    MYLA
          I'll drink anything we can find
          that isn't plain old bottled
          water.  I'm so sick of bottled
          water.  I miss bubbles.

                    RIM
          I can make bubbles in your water.

                    MYLA
          Ew, not those kind.

They laugh.  Eat feed each other more and then grow quiet.

                    RIM
          I wonder what it's really like
          outside.

                    MYLA
          Not sure.  The monitor still shows
          radiation.

                    RIM
          We're out of food.  Water is about
          out too.

                    MYLA
          Time to start recycling.

                    RIM
          You don't mean... ew.  I think I'd
          rather deal with the radiation.

They are quiet a minute and finish the food.

                    MYLA
          Thank you for sharing.

                    RIM
          Of course.  I always do.

                    MYLA
          You've always shared everything
          with me.

                    RIM
          You're my favorite person.  I
          wanted to give you the best of
          everything... and the best of me.

                    MYLA
          You always did... and you stayed
          with me to the end.

                    RIM
          It's not the end... not yet.

                    MYLA
          I remember when they said the bombs
          were coming... I was all alone.

                    RIM
          I was terrified we wouldn't be
          together.

                    MYLA
          Everyone was driving out of the
          city, trying to get far away from
          targets.

                    RIM
          I was driving the other way.

                    MYLA
          They wanted to arrest you... force
          you to go.

                         RIM
          Nothing was going to keep me from
          you.

                         MYLA
          I wasn't going in the shelter
          without you.

                         RIM
          I remember I found you on the
          porch, sitting and looking up at
          the sky.

                         MYLA
          I wondered what it would have
          looked like... all the missiles in
          the sky.

                         RIM
          I crashed the car in to that big
          tree in the yard.

                         MYLA
          I was so glad you weren't
          hurt.  You scared me.

                         RIM
          I was in a hurry.  No time for
          brakes.

                         MYLA
          That would have been an ironic
          ending to your trip home.  Crashing
          and dying.

                         RIM
          I didn't have a scratch on me.

                         MYLA
          We were meant to be mole people
          together.

                         RIM
          Burrowed together in our little
          nest.

                         MYLA
          I like our little nest.

                         RIM
          I think I've been happier here than
          I've ever been before.

                                              (CONTINUED)

                    MYLA
Me too.

                    RIM
No interruptions.  No problems at
work.  No outsiders getting their
noses in our business.

                    MYLA
I never wanted to go outside again.

                    RIM
Except for the last can.

                    MYLA
We made it over a year.

                    RIM
I could go longer.

                    MYLA
Me too.

                    RIM
I wonder what the chair tastes
like.

RIM goes to the chair.

                    MYLA
That's my favorite chair!  You're
not eating that.

RIM removes the cushion.

                    MYLA (CONT.)
What are you doing?

                    RIM
Seeing if you dropped any food down
here.

                    MYLA
You should check your sofa.  I'm a
much cleaner eater than you.

                    RIM
What?

                    MYLA
You need a bib.  That's why I feed
you so you don't make a mess.

>                    RIM
>          Dang... you're right... no food
>          here.

RIM goes to the sofa and removes the cushion.

>                    RIM (CONT.)
>          Jackpot.

>                    MYLA
>          Told you.

>                    RIM
>          Ha... veggie chips... I love these.

>                    MYLA
>          Bon appetit.

>                    RIM
>          Merci.

RIM muches on some veggie chips.

>                    MYLA
>          How many are down there?

>                    RIM
>          A year's supply I think.

>                    MYLA
>          You wish.

>                    RIM
>          If wishes were fishes...

>                    MYLA
>          What does that mean?

>                    RIM
>          No clue.

They laugh.  Rim is munching on veggie chips.  They grow
quiet.  Myla sits in her favorite chair.

>                    MYLA
>          So what do we do?

>                    RIM
>          Go outside?

>                    MYLA
>          But the radiation.

(CONTINUED)

                    RIM
          We might have to risk it.

                    MYLA
          I wonder what it looks like
          outside.

                    RIM
          Maybe all the bombs missed and it's
          all the same as before.

                    MYLA
          Then how do you explain the
          radiation?

                    RIM
          You left the microwave on?

                    MYLA
          Maybe.

They laugh.  Myla is looking at a map now.

                    MYLA (CONT.)
          I wonder where we go?

                    RIM
          Where was the last radio broadcast
          we heard?

                    MYLA
          That was awhile ago.  I think I
          marked it on the map.

                    RIM
          Some little station out in the
          boonies wasn't it?

                    MYLA
          Who would have thought that the
          last bits of civilization would be
          in some little town in the middle
          of nowhere?

                    RIM
          Nowhere became the only somewhere.

                    MYLA
          I wonder how many people from the
          city went there?

>           RIM
> I bet there wasn't enough food to
> go around.

>           MYLA
> Scary.  What are the survivors
> going to do for food?

>           RIM
> Maybe we don't want to go out
> there.

>           MYLA
> I know I don't want to.

They are quiet.

>           RIM
> I wonder how our shoes would
> taste?  Didn't Charlie Chaplin do
> that in a movie?

>           MYLA
> I don't know any Chaplin.  Heard of
> him of course.

>           RIM
> I'm amazed how many movies you do
> know.  It's kept me pretty
> entertained.

>           MYLA
> Want me to perform another movie
> for you?

Rim laughs.

>           RIM
> I think Jurrasic Park is my
> favorite.  You do all the dinosaur
> actions too.

>           MYLA
> I watched that one a lot as a kid.

>           RIM
> I'm still amazed how well you
> memorized them all.

>           MYLA
> One of my many special useless
> skills.

                    RIM
Sure came in handy now.

                    MYLA
I guess it did, didn't it?

                    RIM
You've kept me very entertained.

                    MYLA
I love what you wrote for me.

                    RIM
I love what you drew for me.

                    MYLA
It's probably been the most
creative time in my life.

                    RIM
Me too.  I wonder if anyone will
ever see anything we did.

                    MYLA
It doesn't matter.  I did it for
you.

                    RIM
You're very sweet to me.  I can't
imagine a better person to spend my
life with.

                    MYLA
To be stuck with?

                    RIM
I never felt stuck... even before
we became mole people... you were
the best choice I ever made.

                    MYLA
You're very sweet to me.

                    RIM
You make me feel sweeter... I've
never felt so happy.

                    MYLA
You've always taken good care of
me.

                    RIM
          I never wanted to fail you.

                    MYLA
          You never did.

                    RIM
          Until today...

Myla goes to him.

                    MYLA
          What do you mean?

                    RIM
          The food... it's gone.

                    MYLA
          But we probably had more food than
          anyone else.  You prepared so much
          better than everyone else.  You
          always had everything covered...
          you always took care of
          everything.

                    RIM
          This is the first time I don't know
          what to do.  I never felt like this
          before.

                    MYLA
          Like what?

                    RIM
          Like I didn't know what to do...
          how to solve the problem.

                    MYLA
          Maybe it's time you let someone
          else handle everything.

                    RIM
          You have a plan?

                    MYLA
          No, but I bet someone else does.

Myla points up.

                    RIM
          Oh... I've always admired your
          faith.

>                    MYLA
> We've done well so far.

>                    RIM
> We have.

>                    MYLA
> I have a feeling something is going
> to happen.  Something good.

>                    RIM
> You know... I believe you.  I
> really believe you.

>                    MYLA
> I don't know what or how... but
> something good will happen.

>                    RIM
> I believe.

>                    MYLA
> Then close your eyes and get on
> your knees.

>                    RIM
> We're going to pray.

>                    MYLA
> Yes, pray.

Rim gets down on his knees at the coffee table.  He closes
his eyes and prays silently.  Myla sneaks off.

>                    RIM
> I know I don't pray as often as a I
> should, but I really want to know,
> more than ever... rather than
> begging for something... I want to
> thank you for giving us this
> wonderful year together... I'm so
> thankful we got to be with each
> other... you've given me this
> wonderful gift and she is the most
> precious gift I've even been
> given... I thank you for her... I
> thank you with all my heart.

Myla has come back during this and smiles so happily at his
words.  She places a box of donut cake type things in front
of him.

                                            (CONTINUED)

                         RIM (CONT.)
              Amen.

He opens his eyes and sees her smiling happily and she
points to the box.  Rim laughs.

                         RIM (CONT.)
              You're an angel.

Rim hugs her happily.

                         MYLA
              I saved the best for last.

Suddenly music is heard.

                         RIM
              Do you hear that?

                         MYLA
              That's the intercom.

                         RIM
              It's picking up music from outside.
              Someone's playing music.

                         MYLA
              Beautiful, beautiful music.

                         RIM
              Should we go see?

                         MYLA
              Maybe they're after our Diddly
              Doos?

                         RIM
              Nothing is getting my Diddly Doos.

Myla gets a pouty face.

                         RIM (CONT.)
              Except you of course.

She smiles happily.  The music gets louder.

                         MYLA
              It's coming closer.

                         RIM
              I feel like a kid hearing an ice
              cream truck.

                         MYLA
          Maybe it is an ice cream truck.

                         RIM
          I like Diddly Doos better.

                         MYLA
          Yummy... ice cream.

                         RIM
          Should we go see?

                         MYLA
          Okay.

                         RIM
          Ready?

                         MYLA
          Let me get my sweater.

She gets her sweater.

                         RIM
          Ah... that's such a cute sweater.

                         MYLA
          Thank you.

                         RIM
          Ready?

                         MYLA
          I'm a little scared.

                         RIM
          I'll be with you.

                         MYLA
          Promise.

                         RIM
          I promise. I'll never leave you.

                         MYLA
          You never do.

                         RIM
          Let's go.

They go off stage and sounds of a massive door unlocking and
opening.  Music gets much louder.  After a moment, Rim
rushes back in and gets the box of donut/cake things and
then runs off again.

END OF SCENE

* * * * * * * * * *

PART 18


"END THE HURTING"

A face appears in the darkness.  The face is sad and looks
in pain.

                          ME
          When you're hurting you look for
          weakness.
          You take that hurt and pass it on
          to me.  You're hurting... so you
          hurt
          .  You're damaged... so you damage
          .  You're feeling pain so you cause
          pain... in me
          .

(The light becomes brighter and the face transforms looking
stronger and determined.)

                       ME (CONT.)
          It has to stop
          .  I will protect myself from the
          pain
          .  I know the damage must be undone
          .  I will end the hurting so I
          never hurt.
          And I must do it... for me.

                    * * * * * * * * * *

                      END OF PLAY

                    * * * * * * * * * *

CAST

Actors can play multiple roles.  At least 8 actors are
needed for the production with at least 2 females and 2
males.  The cast can be as large as 40.

                    * * * * * * * * * *

INDEX

The play includes the following scenes:


                                                   (CONTINUED)

Printed in Great Britain
by Amazon